This book is dedicated to all who cherish America's history as a vast heritage of people and events— some heroic, some inglorious, but all part of America's epic struggle to come of age—and to all who know that understanding the past is essential to dealing with the present.

CABRILLO
THE STORY BEHIND THE SCENERY®

by Dr. Raymond Starr
Photography by Richard Cummins

Dr. Raymond Starr, Professor Emeritus of History of San Diego State University, has written *San Diego: A Pictorial History* (1985), *San Diego State University: A History in Word and Image* (1995), and numerous articles and reviews on the region. Since 1980 he has been a frequent trustee (and twice chair) of the Cabrillo National Monument Foundation.

Richard Cummins is an internationally published photographer and writer. An Irishman by birth, he and his wife emigrated to Southern California in 1989 after serving ten years in the Irish Lighthouse Service. Now a U.S. citizen, he is a self-taught photographer who is represented by major stock agencies in the United States, Europe, and Australia.

Cabrillo National Monument, *located in southern California, was established in 1913 to commemorate Juan Rodríguez Cabrillo, and also preserves the Old Point Loma Lighthouse and the coastal sage scrub environment.*

Edited by Cheri C. Madison. Book design by K.C. DenDooven.

CABRILLO: THE STORY BEHIND THE SCENERY. © 2001 KC PUBLICATIONS, INC.
"The Story Behind the Scenery"; the parallelogram forms and colors within are registered in the U.S. Patent and Trademark Office.
ISBN 0-88714-217-6.

Cabrillo National Monument is one of the National Park Service's jewels. It is a small monument located on a peninsula that juts out into the sea and sky in San Diego, California. In addition to offering spectacular views of the region's mountains, the Pacific Ocean, the Coronado Islands, and the cities of San Diego and Tijuana, it also has historical attractions commemorating the first Spanish contact with the region, the history of lighthouses and navigation, and modern American military installations. One of the last refuges of coastal sage scrub habitat, it offers unique fauna and flora, and fragile tidepools along its western shore. From its heights, one can watch the annual migration of the Pacific gray whales as they move south from Alaska. It has a visitor center, several museums, trails, a whale-watching outlook, and a series of programs to entertain and inform the visitor. From a very unimpressive beginning in 1913, Cabrillo National Monument has become an informative and delightful place.

The Monument is located at the tip of a high peninsula, whose cliffs provide visual beauty as well as tidepools and habitat for a variety of land and shore life.

Cabrillo and a Lighthouse

Although Cabrillo National Monument was created in 1913 to commemorate the first Spanish expedition to the area, for years little was done to tell that story. Instead, the Monument focused on the remains of an 1855 lighthouse.

Cabrillo National Monument was caused by the Panama Canal. As construction neared completion of that connector of oceans, the little city of San Diego (with a population of less than 40,000) planned a series of events to remind the world that it was the first American port heading north out of the canal. The town fathers hoped this would make San Diego the big city they had been planning for since the 1850s.

To create that attention they launched a world's fair, the 1915-1916 Panama-California Exposition, which was built around a Mediterranean theme, with a heavy use of Spanish history and myth. Accompanying that was a flurry of construction in Spanish and Mission revival architecture throughout the town, the renaming of City Park as Balboa Park, and some early restoration work on some Spanish-Mexican era historical sites. To top it all off, San Diego wanted to construct a huge statue of Juan Rodríguez Cabrillo on Point Loma, the peninsula that guarded entry into San Diego Bay. In their request for the site, the San Diegan leaders noted, in the Eurocentric manner of the day, that Point Loma had been "the first land ever seen by a civilized man on the Pacific verge of the United States."

Cabrillo was chosen as the subject of the dominating monument because he had been the commander of the first Spanish expedition to the area, and because he exemplified the adventurous spirit of the Spanish conquistadors who spread that country's influence throughout most of the Western Hemisphere.

This medallion was struck in 1913, the same *year the Monument was created, to honor the leader of the first European expedition to explore the coast of California. The medallion was part of a larger program of using the region's Spanish heritage to promote an image and identity of San Diego.*

The charm and beauty of the Old Point Loma Lighthouse made it a visitor attraction long before Cabrillo National Monument was created. Restored to its 1880s appearance, it has always been a popular part of the Monument, as well as a defining symbol of the region, used frequently today on logos and signs.

We know relatively little about Cabrillo. He may have been born in Portugal, although some modern scholars doubt that. There is no likeness of him, so we can only guess what he looked like. We do know he began service with the Spanish in Cuba and played a significant role in Hernán Cortés's conquest of Mexico between 1519 and 1521. In preparing the major counterattack that secured the Spanish conquest of the Aztecs, Cortés made Cabrillo supervisor of native workers to prepare tallow and sap to seal and protect the planks of a fleet of 13 brigantines that Cortés ordered built for the attack. After the Spanish secured Mexico City, they moved southward.

Over the next few years, Cabrillo played a significant role in the Spanish conquest of southern Mexico and Guatemala, and was rewarded with the status of *hidalgo*, grants of lands (and their inhabitants), and gold mines, which made him a substantial figure in colonial Guatemala. He also built ships and began to engage in trade. He married a native woman and had three daughters; then, in keeping with his status as an *hidalgo*, he went back to Spain for a Spanish bride with a proper pedigree, and started another family.

When the Spanish authorities decided in the 1540s to send voyages of exploration up the West Coast of the North American continent and across the Pacific, they chose Cabrillo to lead the North American expedition. Thus, on June 27, 1542, Cabrillo departed from the Mexican port of Navidad with three ships and about 200 people to explore and chart the western coast of North America. After slowly working their way up the coast of Mexico, on September 28, 1542, they pulled into "an enclosed harbor which was very good," which they named San Miguel; it was later renamed San Diego. In that harbor they interacted with local inhabitants. This was the first known landing of a European on the West Coast of the

Richard DeRosset's depiction of Cabrillo's flagship, San Salvador, *represents an educated guess as to what it looked like—we have no contemporary pictures of it. Called a "galleon," it was most likely about 100 feet long and 25 feet wide, had both rectangular and triangular sails, and could carry about 200 tons of cargo as well as a crew of about 100. The expedition also included two smaller vessels,* Victoria *and* San Miguel.

present-day United States, and it was to honor that event that Cabrillo National Monument was created in 1913.

After five days, Cabrillo and his men continued explorations up the coast, possibly as far as modern Oregon. The expedition returned to Navidad on April 14, 1543, but without Cabrillo, who had died after an injury. As a result, the Spanish now claimed most of the West Coast of North America, and the San Diego region entered into the consciousness of the western world. In 1769, Spain established the settlement that became the modern city of San Diego—making it the first European town in the present-day state of California.

It was to honor Cabrillo, his expedition, and the Spanish era that followed, that the city fathers proposed the statue on Point Loma. The land they

needed had been a federal military reserve since 1852 so San Diego approached Washington, D. C., about the matter. On October 14, 1913, President Woodrow Wilson signed a proclamation setting aside half an acre of land surrounding an old lighthouse as Cabrillo National Monument.

But nothing happened. The statue project fizzled and the Monument remained under the control of the army. In 1926 President Calvin Coolidge transferred the rights to build the statue to the Order of the Golden West, a group dedicated to celebrating California's heritage. But nothing came of that, either.

Things changed only after 1933 when Cabrillo National Monument was transferred to the National Park Service, which initially placed it under the control of Sequoia National Park. The Monument secured independent status in 1956.

The spectacular view of San Diego and the mountains behind *it is a major reason why Cabrillo National Monument is one of the most popular sites in the National Park System, with over a million visitors per year. A recent survey showed that 63 percent of visitors gave the view as the main reason they visited the Monument.*

JAMES BLANK

Except for dedicating a plaque to Cabrillo in 1935, the National Park Service did next to nothing to interpret the man for whom the Monument was named. They did, however, begin to care for and make available the Old Point Loma Lighthouse—which remains a primary focus of Cabrillo National Monument.

The Point Loma Lighthouse

The Point Loma lighthouse began operation in 1855 as one of eight lighthouses the United States government built on the Pacific coast to aid navigation. The government was seeking to encourage American entrepreneurial capitalism in the region it had acquired from Mexico as a result of the 1848 Treaty of Guadalupe Hidalgo. The lighthouse oper-

ated until 1891 when it was replaced because cloud banks frequently obscured the light.

The lighthouse consisted of a sandstone structure topped with a brick tower housing a third order Fresnel lens. There also were an assistant keeper's quarters, a barn and oil storage shed, two cisterns (plus a third in the basement), and a garden to supply the keeper, his family, and his assistant.

During its period of operation, 1855-1891, the lighthouse and its keepers and families were an integral part of the community. The best known of the keepers was Robert Israel, who served as principal keeper from 1873 until the lighthouse closure in 1891; it is that period the Monument uses for its present-day restoration and interpretation of the lighthouse.

Although the main purpose of the lighthouse
*structure was to house the lens and necessary
supplies, it also served as the home of the
keeper and his family. The parlor, kitchen, and two
bedrooms have been restored to illustrate life
in the 1880s, and provide insights into the lifestyles
of both lighthouse keepers and Americans in
general during that period.*

This 11,000-gallon cistern was built
*in 1883 to supplement a 1,240-gallon
cistern in the basement and collection in casks
of runoff from the roof. In years with little rainfall,
even this failed to meet the lighthouse's needs
and the keeper had to haul 50-gallon barrels of
water from wells seven miles away.*

After the light was replaced in 1891, the structure languished without repairs, was occupied by soldiers, and was visited by local residents on outings. The structure emerged as a visual landmark defining the community, and appeared on many tourist postcards, usually incorrectly labeled as the "Old Spanish Lighthouse." After the transfer of the Monument to the National Park Service, the lighthouse—as the only structure on the half-acre Monument—became the focus of some attention. The Park Service built a comfort station, repaired the building, and used it as headquarters and visitor center of the Monument until the mid-1960s when the current Visitor Center was opened.

The Park Service soon began serious work toward documenting and preserving the lighthouse. It had the building documented for the Historic American Building Survey, and used that information for a major, thorough restoration, which was completed by 1935. The work was done under auspices of the Depression-era Works Progress Administration, and thus that restoration itself has become a part of American history. Additional major restoration work was done in 1984, when the administration had the building refurbished, a more authentic wood roof installed, and the proper lenses installed in the tower. In 1995 the Monument staff refurnished the structure with items appropriate to the 1880s. In 2000, plans were underway to restore the grounds around the house to their original setting.

That restored structure is the building which visitors see today. It is furnished as it was between 1871-1891, and the Monument staff interprets the light and the life of its keepers in many ways. It is, in the minds and eyes of many visitors and residents of the region, the crown of Cabrillo National Monument.

Juan Rodriguez Cabrillo

Although the Monument was named after Cabrillo, little was done in the beginning to memorialize the explorer. An eight-foot-high bronze plaque was dedicated in 1935 and installed north of the lighthouse. In the 1940s, the Monument "acquired" (some say "stole") a large statue of Cabrillo and installed it on the Monument grounds.

Portuguese sculptor Alvaro DeBree had executed a 14-foot-high statue of Cabrillo as a gift for the 1939 San Francisco world's fair. It never made it to the fair, and the governor of California awarded it to the city of Oakland—although, in fact, it ended up stored in a private garage. When San Diego State Senator Ed Fletcher heard this, he engineered a "liberation" of the statue—and its removal by truck and train to San Diego. In 1949 it was placed next to the lighthouse, and the Monument finally had at least a visual depiction of its namesake. In 1966 the Park Service moved the statue to a prominent position overlooking San Diego and the site where Cabrillo probably first landed in 1542.

The importance of the Cabrillo story to the community of San Diego has been shown by periodic celebrations honoring the explorer. The first were Cabrillo Festivals held in 1892 and 1894, when San Diego began to use its Hispanic past to create a unique identity for itself. In the 1930s, there were Cabrillo Days—and in 1964 the modern Cabrillo Festival was born.

Held at the Monument every year, the Cabrillo Festival includes social activities, ethnic programs, and a recreation of Cabrillo's landing in San Diego Bay, as well as official ceremonies. Dominated for years by the Portuguese community, the commemorations now include Spanish, Mexican, and Native American participation. The National Park Service sees the Festival as a major aspect of its interpretation of the Cabrillo story.

In addition, since the opening of the Visitor Center in 1966, the Monument has had a museum to explain and interpret Cabrillo and Spanish explorations in the New World. Many summers the Monument presents a live dramatization of the Cabrillo story, and periodic living history activities.

The matter of Cabrillo statues has remained an issue at the Monument. In 1967 San Diego's mayor, Frank Curran, revived the 1913 idea of a 150-foot-high statue at the Monument. To the relief of many, the plan was defeated. On the other hand, by the 1970s the 1939 DeBree statue of Cabrillo, which had been made of a soft sandstone, had begun to deterio-

The 14-foot-high limestone statue of *Juan Rodríguez Cabrillo, shown with San Diego city lights in the background, is one of several ways in which the Monument memorializes its namesake.*

rate badly. It clearly needed replacing. With help from a major donor, several organizations, and the Portuguese government, Monument Superintendent Doris Omundson secured a prominent contemporary Portuguese sculptor, Charters de Almeida, to replicate the statue in Portuguese limestone. It was dedicated in 1988 and now is the primary memorial to Cabrillo in the monument named after him.

The Spanish saw their conquests as much in religious as in political or economic terms; they were sure they were doing God's work. This actor with a cross could be playing Fray Julian de Lescansco, who accompanied Cabrillo's voyage of exploration.

Reenactments and Living History

Historical reenactments and living history performances are among the ways Cabrillo National Monument tells its stories to the public. Visitors may be greeted in the lighthouse by costumed interpreters depicting the lighthouse keeper or his wife. If the wife is there, she may be making pickles or sewing. Sometimes visitors may see a 16th-century Spanish soldier firing an arquebus of the period. Since there are no physical remains of Cabrillo's expedition on the site, the Monument especially uses reenactments to tell his story. Each year the Cabrillo Festival, Inc., with input from the Monument, reenacts Cabrillo's landing in San Diego Bay. During part of the year, the Monument presents an original drama depicting the Cabrillo voyage.

Mike Love, a Volunteer-In-Parks (VIP) dressed as a conquistador of the 16th century, is typical of the "living history" which a visitor might encounter at the Monument. He is showing visitors an example of a Spanish sword and explaining the role of weaponry in the Spanish exploration and conquest of the Americas.

This handsome stylized (and probably not very accurate) bronze model of Cabrillo's flagship, San Salvador, greets visitors at the entry to the Monument. Like the lighthouse, it is frequently used as a symbol of the Monument.

These actors are depicting a sailor aboard Cabrillo's ship, the expedition's priest, and two local Indians. They remind us that Cabrillo's visit to the area in 1542 represented the first encounter between Europeans and Native Americans in the region. Since there are no physical remnants in the Monument to illustrate that encounter, dramatic presentations are an excellent way to convey that part of the Cabrillo story.

The keeper's bedroom was furnished more modestly than the parlor downstairs. For instance, the bed was pine painted to look like oak; it also deviated from the usual style of a bedstead for the period, because it had to have a low headboard to fit under the sloping ceiling. The lady's hatpins and toilet set on the dresser reflect the grand dress styles of even the lower-middle-class women of the 1880s.

The kitchen was both the "family room" and a place to eat. Food was always a challenge, since it was too dry to grow much of a garden, and too far to go to the nearest food store. The lighthouse service did provide each keeper with an annual allotment of pork, beef, flour, rice, brown sugar, coffee, beans, and two barrels of potatoes.

The Keeper

Lighthouses the size of San Diego's were staffed by a keeper and an assistant keeper. The keepers operated according to detailed instructions, and after 1884, wore uniforms. Generally turnover was very high, as pay was low ($1,000 a year for the keeper and $650 for the assistant), the lighthouse isolated, and the work very routine. Thus in its 36 years of operation, the Point Loma lighthouse had 11 keepers and 21 assistant keepers. The San Diego situation was unique, however, in that one keeper, Robert D. Israel, served for nearly 20 years. Israel began as an assistant keeper and moved up in 1873; when the light was moved in 1891, he moved with it. Married to Maria Arcadia Alipas, descendant of a prominent San Diego family, he had four sons. Some of his descendants still live in the area, and have been very helpful in restoring the lighthouse interiors.

It is easy for the visitor to the lighthouse to forget that this was a government establishment, and the keeper a government bureaucrat, with forms and accounts to be filed, and correspondence to be attended to. Those activities undoubtedly took place at a desk like this one tucked into the corner of the parlor.

A coal-burning stove was used for cooking food and for heat, which probably made the kitchen a cozy family center during the cool, damp Point Loma days and nights. Fuel, like water, was a major problem here, but the lighthouse service provided an annual ration of coal and firewood.

The Light

The Point Loma lighthouse was equipped with the latest and best lens available at the time. Developed in the 1820s by Frenchman Augustin Fresnel, the lens was like a glass barrel with a variety of prisms and a bulls-eye on the outside, and a light in the inside. The light, when focused through the prisms and bulls-eye, radiated out in steady beams. Local legend says the San Diego light was fueled by whale oil from locally harvested whales. That could not be true, as the lamps used sperm whale oil, and sperm whales did not inhabit local waters. By the 1880s, whale and other oil was replaced by kerosene.

This National Park Service volunteer, Howard Burdett, *is duplicating one of the jobs of the lighthouse keeper. Regulations demanded that the light be prepared by "10 o'clock, a.m., daily." That included cleaning and polishing the lens and the glass of the tower, cleaning and filling the lamp, and polishing all the brass and copper parts. While doing this, keepers had to wear linen aprons to prevent their coarse clothes from scratching the lens.*

This lighthouse served the needs
of seafarers sailing in and out of
San Diego Bay from its first lighting in
1855 to its replacement in 1891.
The light remained dark until the National
Park Service re-lit it in 1984. This is
how it may have looked to the keeper,
his family, and the assistant keeper,
on a clear Point Loma evening—a sight
still enjoyed by San Diegans.

This dramatic view of the Fresnel lens
illustrates the bulls-eye and prisms that
magnified the light of a single lamp. The San
Diego light was designed to be seen at
a distance of 28 miles; there were reports
of it being seen 39 miles at sea.

The Natural World

Cabrillo National Monument preserves one of the few remaining areas of coastal sage scrub habitat, plus tidepools, and both a resident and a migratory bird population.

Cabrillo's unique natural environment is the result of its location on the tip of a relatively isolated peninsula bathed by a damp, mild climate. This has produced the rare coastal sage scrub environment that dominates; the coastline adds intertidal features and an opportunity to interact with the sea.

The sea provides one major aspect of the Monument's life—the observation of the Pacific (sometimes called California) gray whales as they pass the Point during their annual migration from the Arctic Ocean and Bering Sea to Scammon's Lagoon and Magdalena Bay to the south of San

Point Loma was the logical site for a navigational light and for military installations to defend San Diego. The peninsula also offers a variety of natural assets, ranging from sandy beaches and tidepools, to cliffs and coastal sage scrub.

JAMES BLANK

Each year over 90,000 people visit the rocky intertidal area, or tidepools, of Cabrillo National Monument, where they discover some of nature's best instruction in how creatures adapt to their environment.

Point Loma was formed
*when many layers of old
seabed and beach were uplifted to create a peninsula which, today, is over 400 feet high.
The cliffs expose these layers of previous eons (clearly identifiable in this photograph) and
include fossilized sea creatures. Of soft stone, the cliffs are unstable and visitors should
exercise caution around them.*

Diego. The annual whale watch weekend produces crowds of thousands who come to see the whales and learn about them from park rangers and guest speakers.

Likewise, the rocky intertidal area (usually called tidepools) is a colorful and fascinating aspect of the Monument. The tidepools, the area between the high and low tide marks, contain unique life-forms (such as sea cucumbers, urchins, sea stars, and a variety of marine snails and crustaceans) and also are a nursery for the development of a number of deeper ocean forms. Visitors can wade into the pools at low tide and observe the tidal creatures—and an average of 90,000 per year do so. Since 1990, the National Park Service has been monitoring the condition of the tidepools. A drastic decline in several key species has led to steps to improve the viability of this fragile ecosystem, and to educate the public about its condition.

Above the sea, the landmass presents some interesting and easily recognizable geological features. The Point Loma peninsula is a series of old marine terraces lifted up by tectonic plate action as a fault block. The layers of sandstone, mudstone, and gravels can easily be examined on the waterside cliffs of the Monument. They show evidence of the old ocean levels, contain fossils of past plant and animal life, and help the visitor understand the origins of this part of the earth.

This uplifted landmass is mostly covered by coastal sage scrub habitat, which used to be commonplace in coastal California, but which now remains in only a few places. This environment features no large trees—rather, it is dominated by California sagebrush supplemented by about 270 other species, including buckwheat, California sunflowers, other sages, lemonade berry, toyon, and sumac. A unique characteristic of Cabrillo's coastal sage scrub is the presence of a number of succulents, such as chalk live-forever, San Diego barrel cactus, and fishhook and cholla cactuses. These plants reflect various fascinating adaptations to their environment. They also often played a role in the human history of the region, providing foodstuffs, clothing, medicines, and household goods.

Unfortunately, the natural coastal sage scrub on Point Loma has been invaded by many non-native plants, called "exotics." The most common ones are acacia, several species of the ground cover commonly called "ice plant," eucalyptus, Natal plum, and myoporum. To restore and preserve the natural habitat, the Monument has been aggressively removing exotics and replacing them with native plants.

The San Diego barrel cactus is common in the Monument. Ubiquitous in the region, barrel cacti are so appreciated that it is difficult to protect them from poachers.

Cholla cactus is part of the coastal sage scrub habitat. Its sharp, penetrating thorns protect it from predators.

Sea lavender, whose light purple blossoms are a common sight from July to December, is native to the region. Variations with yellow, white, or blue flowers are European imports.

The Mojave yucca is found throughout the southwestern United States and northern Mexico and features creamy white flowers in the spring. It was a valued plant for local Kumeyaay Indians, who used its fibers for sandals, woven ropes, mats, and even clothing. The roots were ground up and used as soap for washing. The Kumeyaay had a use for most native plants on Point Loma.

The common raven is one of the birds frequently seen (perched on a bush or soaring like a hawk) or heard (they make a coarse cr-r-ruck sound) at the Monument.

The California ground squirrel is often seen, to the delight of visitors at Cabrillo, but their burrows can cause erosion of the soft cliffs.

WILDLIFE

These plants and the sea around the Monument provide cover and food for a very large number of birds. Over 350 species have been sighted and identified here. They include sea-related birds like osprey, terns, and pelicans—and birds attracted to the chaparral environment, such as several species of hummingbirds, hawks, ravens, and kestrels. Peregrine falcons also nest in the region. Since San Diego lies under one of the nation's major migratory bird flyways, the Monument is visited every year by waves of migrants, such as the gray flycatcher; sage thrasher; red-eyed vireo; Tennessee, Lucy, chestnut-sided, palm, and black-and-white warblers; the flammulated owl; various tanagers; the orchard oriole; and many others.

For such a small area surrounded by the sea and the city, Cabrillo is home to a surprising variety of wildlife. There are the expected gray foxes, California ground squirrels, and coyotes, some of which are occasionally seen by staff and visitors. In addition, there are such animals as California voles, cactus mice, desert cottontails, and raccoons. Beyond mammals, the Monument also hosts many reptiles and amphibians, such as snakes, lizards, and salamanders. An herpetological study of those

One of the grander sights on Point Loma is the brown pelican,
majestic in flight, sleek and efficient as it dives into the water for its
meal, or rather comical perched on a stump. Native to the region, brown pelicans almost became extinct because
of pollution. When the pesticide DDT was banned, the pelicans made a dramatic comeback.

creatures has been documenting their presence and number, thus providing data for conservation. Among the findings have been the expected— Southern Pacific rattlesnakes; striped racers; western fence, alligator, and side-blotched lizards—and a few surprises, such as the orange-throated whip-tail lizard.

After United States Navy transfers of land increased the area of Cabrillo National Monument to about 160 acres covering most of the tip of the Point Loma peninsula, the natural setting became a very important aspect of the Monument. It is a special resource, as illustrated by the presence of several threatened and endangered species and dozens of other rare plant and animal species. Reflecting this, the Nature Conservancy has declared the coastal California shrublands one of the most imperiled habitats in the nation.

Because of the extent and significance of its natural resources, the Monument staff has been devoting increasing attention to those resources and their interpretation. There is the one-mile-long Bayside Trail, which runs from near the lighthouse to the bayside. It features interpretive markers to help visitors understand the ecology of the coastal sage environment, as well as some military sites on the lower trail. The staff has also placed identifying labels near many species of plant life throughout the Monument.

Perhaps the most exciting aspect of the National Park Service's role to preserve our natural heritage has been its participation in the Point Loma Ecological Reserve. The preserve was created in 1995 by several U. S. Navy commands, the National Park Service, United States Coast Guard, Department of Veterans Affairs, and the City of San Diego to set aside conservation areas and corridors to preserve the unique coastal chaparral environment on Point Loma.

The popularity of the tidepools has created a challenge for the National Park Service. How do you allow people to enjoy this fragile resource while preserving it for future generations? As a result of innovative research, the Park Service closed part of the tidepools to allow them to recover from the damage caused by heavy visitation. It also stations rangers and volunteers in the tidepools to protect them and to answer visitor questions.

Harbor seals (not to be confused with the larger California sea lion) can sometimes be seen and heard on the rocky shores of Point Loma. They retreat to the nearby Channel Islands or Coronado Islands in spring to bear and raise their young.

Tidepool Life

Cabrillo National Monument contains one of the finest rocky intertidal areas (often called "tidepools") on the southern California coast. The rocky intertidal is the area between the highest and the lowest tides. It is divided into three zones—low, middle, and high—each of which sustains unique life-forms. The low zone is covered by water except for the very lowest of tides, and features marine life such as seaweed and surfgrass, chitons, sea urchins, and sponges. By contrast, the high intertidal zone is only covered by the highest tides and includes things which can live long periods out of water, such as a variety of snails, barnacles, limpets, and crabs. Most of the tidepools at Cabrillo are in the middle zone, which features many small pools left at low tide. In this zone one might find shrimp, sea anemones, sea hares, and a variety of small fish. Life in each zone is primarily defined by the ways in which it adapts to its changing environment.

The lined shore crab is one of the residents of the middle and high intertidal zones. Visitors often see them scurrying around looking for food in and among the rocks. They are easily frightened and will quickly seek protection in a crevice or under a rock. It is probably good that they are timid, because they are a favorite food of seagulls.

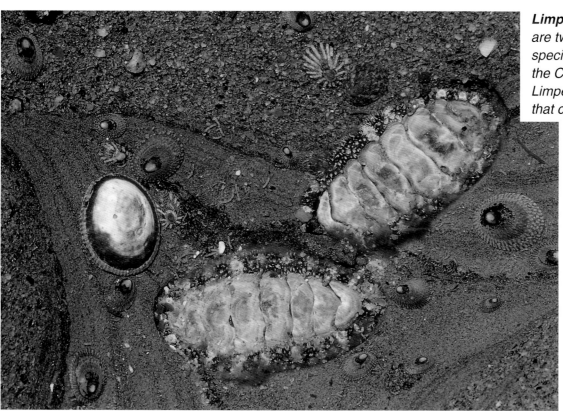

Limpets and chitons are two algae-eating species easily found in the Cabrillo tidepools. Limpets are shellfish that can be found clinging to rocks in the high intertidal zone. Chitons are mollusks covered with eight plates, which usually attach themselves to rocks and graze on the algae.

Watching Pacific *gray whales migrate south each winter is an exciting event at Cabrillo. To facilitate visitor viewing, the Monument has built a Whale Overlook with exhibits and audio interpretations. It also includes a statue of a whale, with labeling in Braille, to help sight-impaired visitors visualize these mammals.*

Cabrillo National *Monument is somewhat unique among National Park areas in that it is one of the few national parks or monuments located in a major urban center. It provides a quiet refuge where local residents and visitors alike can get away from the noise and stress of the sixth largest city in the nation.*

The 1891 lighthouse is still in use. Since it is fully automated, the houses built for the keepers are now occupied by high-ranking officers of the United States Coast Guard. The Coast Guard operates the light, and conducts search and rescue and law enforcement operations in the waters around San Diego.

The U.S. Coast Guard and the Lighthouse

Although the l855 lighthouse was beloved by San Diegans who made it a tourist attraction long before Cabrillo National Monument was created, it left much to be desired as a navigational aid. The light was 462 feet above sea level, the highest U. S. lighthouse at the time. But its light was often obscured by low clouds and fog. Since there was no foghorn, there are stories that Keeper Robert Israel used to fire a shotgun off the tower to warn ships they were too close to the dangerous shoals. At one point the government ordered the light be cut from three to two wicks, to save fuel worth about $25.00 a year; it also cut the distance the light could be seen by half. Finally, in 1891 a new lighthouse was built at the bottom of the hill. Fully automated, it is operated by the U.S. Coast Guard and continues to welcome sailors to San Diego.

The United States Lighthouse Board replaced the 1855 Point Loma light with a new one located on the tip of the peninsula, only 30 feet above sea level. It was supplemented with a harbor light in 1894. Although an improvement over the old light, the wrecking of the Wallace McDonald in 1909 shows that it was not foolproof.

The Military

Cabrillo National Monument provides several ways to learn how for two centuries, first the Spanish and then the U. S. Army defended San Diego, a "harbor worth defending."

In recent years, the Cabrillo National Monument leadership has turned its attention to preserving the military heritage of the site. The Monument had been carved out of Fort Rosecrans, which was on a military reserve that had been set aside in 1852. Thus, the land that is now the Monument has seen significant aspects of the American military experience, and many reminders of that experience are still visible. The National Park Service has added the military experience to the interpretive charge of Cabrillo National Monument, and much has been done to make that military experience accessible to the visitor.

The military has played a key role on Point Loma since the Spanish era. It was especially important during World War II. An exhibit, housed in a World War I era radio station, uses photos, captions, videos, and artifacts (including a 16-inch shell which could be fired 25 miles) to explain the role of the U. S. Army's coast defense system from 1936 to 1947, with special emphasis on the 19th Coastal Artillery.

This installation, just below the Whale Overlook, was the battery commander station and a fire control (also called base-end) station for one of the huge World War II guns, Battery Humphrey, located just south of Battery Bluff. This was one of 13 batteries operating on the Point during World War II. Their firepower ranged from machine guns to major 16-inch artillery pieces.

Military roots on the site go deep. Considering the nature of the Monument's location—a peninsula overlooking the only entry into San Diego Bay—it was inevitable that the peninsula would become a significant military site. The Spanish had recognized this and in the 1790s built a fortification, *El Castillo de San Joaquin* (popularly known as Fort Guijarros), on the bayside of the peninsula. It guarded entry to the bay into the Mexican period, falling into ruin in the 1830s. The United States set the peninsula aside for the military reserve just a few years after acquiring the area from Mexico. For a long time after that, nothing happened.

In the 1870s and 1880s the United States started plans to fortify the peninsula, but the plans were not implemented. In 1896 Congress finally appropriated money and the first major defensive batteries followed, including Batteries McGrath, Fetterman, Wilkeson, and Meed, on the bayside of the Point. A military cemetery was also set aside. The United States began to station troops on the reservation, which was named Fort Rosecrans in 1899.

In the years that followed, a variety of structures were built on the fort, along with continual modernization of the gun emplacements. Fort Rosecrans served several functions—most notably the first line of defense against invasion of San Diego. It also became the home of the Coast Artillery, which used Fort Rosecrans's guns to train

many of the American artillerymen who fought in World War I. After that war, the military establishment languished, to be restored with the growing threat of the second world war.

That led to construction of massive new batteries on the ocean side of the peninsula to defend the town from battleships miles off shore. These batteries, some of which can be seen on the road into the Monument, included Ashburn, Humphries, Whistler, Strong, Point Loma, and White. The batteries themselves were supplemented by "base-end stations," which were used to provide data for aiming the guns; plus searchlights, and—after World War II began—anti-aircraft guns and beach defenses. Fort Rosecrans also provided defense of the entry to the harbor with a system of mines and nets. After 1945, the changed nature of war made the installations on Point Loma obsolete and most were abandoned. Part of the military establishment was given to the U. S. Navy for a submarine base (visible from the Visitor Center), and most of the rest of the fort was turned over to various research facilities.

NPS PHOTO

This is what would have been happening inside a World War II fire control station. Artillerymen used sophisticated scopes and mathematical charts to pinpoint a target. That information was forwarded to a battery commander station, where it was correlated with sightings from other control stations to determine the exact setting for aiming the guns. As it turned out, the enemy never threatened San Diego and none of the guns on Point Loma were ever fired in anger.

Fort Rosecrans National Cemetery, which can easily be visited on the way to or from the Monument, is considered by many as one of the most beautiful military cemeteries in the country. It began in the 1870s as a burial grounds for soldiers from the San Diego Barracks; it now houses the remains of over 65,000 military personnel and their dependents, including those of longtime lighthouse keeper (and veteran) Robert Israel.

Spectacular views of the region are one of Cabrillo National Monument's most dramatic characteristics. Since San Diego is one of the largest naval centers in the world, many of the views focus on naval activity in the region. From the Monument one can see a number of bases, such as the submarine base just below the Visitor Center, and the North Island navy airbase (seen here behind the aircraft carrier Constellation as it enters San Diego Bay). In the bay, there is a continual parade of military vessels and aircraft—large and small, combat and support.

To date Cabrillo National Monument has officially identified 21 military sites on the grounds of the Monument—including gun emplacements, base-end stations, searchlight shelters, a radio station, and generation stations. They are being preserved, and some have been made available for view on the Bayside Trail and at other locations. In 1999 the National Park Service opened a museum devoted to the military on Point Loma. Located in a World War I-era radio station, it stresses the role of the Coast Artillery on the Point.

The recent opening of this museum has rounded out the interpretive mission of Cabrillo National Monument—Cabrillo and Spanish exploration, the lighthouse, and navigation; the natural world; and the military on the Point. Coupled with the facilities of a Visitor Center which opened in 1966 and provides both orientation and spectacular views of San Diego Bay, the city skyline, and many military installations, Cabrillo National Monument, in the 21st century, offers much to the visitor.

The Visitor Center was built in 1965 as part of the National Park Service's national program of improvement, "Mission 66." Designed with a natural/nautical flair, which fits appropriately into its setting, the main visitor center building provides assistance and orientation to visitors, the Cabrillo National Monument Foundation's sales area, and small rotating exhibits. The views toward the city and the naval installations are among the best on Point Loma. In addition, there are an auditorium, a museum interpreting the Cabrillo story, and administrative offices.

SUGGESTED READING

BRANDON, JEFFREY, and FRANK J. ROKOP. *Life Between the Tides: The Natural History of Common Seashore Life of Southern California*. San Diego: American Southwest Publishing Co., 1985.

CABRILLO NATIONAL MONUMENT FOUNDATION. *An Account of the Voyage of Juan Rodríguez Cabrillo*. San Diego: Cabrillo National Monument Foundation, 1999.

GOHIER, FRANCOIS. *A Pod of Gray Whales* (revised ed.). San Luis Obispo, California: EZ Nature Books, 1999.

HOLLAND, F. ROSS. *The Old Point Loma Lighthouse* (revised ed.). San Diego: Cabrillo Historical Association, 1978.

JOYCE, BARRY A. *A Harbor Worth Defending: A Military History of Point Loma*. San Diego: Cabrillo Historical Association, 1995.

LAVENDER, DAVID. *DeSoto, Coronado, Cabrillo: Explorers of The Northern Mystery*. Washington, D. C.: National Park Service, 1992.

WALKER, THEODORE. *Whale Primer* (revised ed.). San Diego: Cabrillo Historical Association, 1985.

This statue of Cabrillo is a replica of the 1939 original. By the 1970s the soft sandstone of the old statue was deteriorating badly, so Monument Superintendent Doris Omundson secured a Portuguese artist who used Portuguese limestone to replicate the statue. After being brought to San Diego in a Portuguese frigate, the new statue was installed in 1988. The original is in storage.

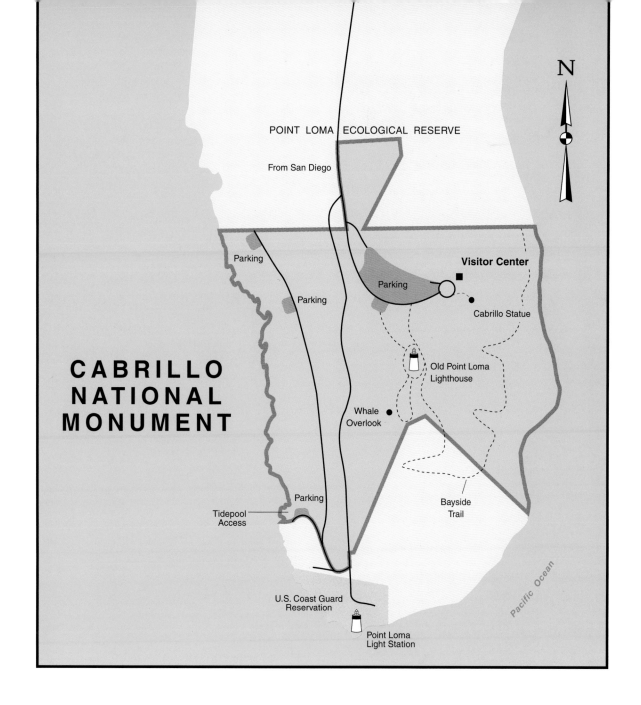

CABRILLO NATIONAL MONUMENT

Cabrillo National Monument, located at the southern tip of Point Loma in San Diego, California, was created by presidential proclamation signed by Woodrow Wilson on October 14, 1913. This 160-acre monument, one of over 380 units of the U.S. National Park System, was established to commemorate the historic voyage of exploration of Juan Rodríguez Cabrillo in 1542-1543. Cabrillo and his men were the first Europeans to discover San Diego Bay and what is now the West Coast of the United States. Today the park protects and preserves unique natural and cultural elements of San Diego and U.S. history. The Monument is open daily from 9:00 AM to 5:15 PM. It is accessible via State Highway 209 and is on Route 26 of the San Diego Metropolitan Transit System.

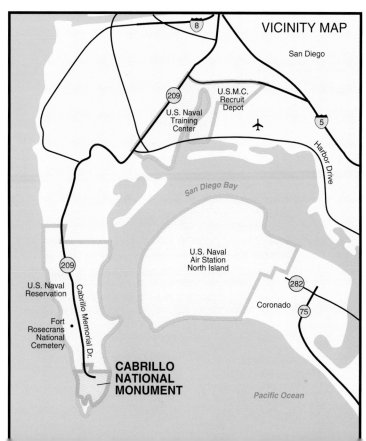

To the Future

If it were nothing more than the place where the land meets the sky and the sea at the entry to San Diego Bay, Cabrillo National Monument would be a special place. When one adds to it the story of Spanish exploration and early contact with Native Americans, one of the first eight lighthouses on the West Coast, and the significant role the Point has played in the military defense of the area, especially during World War II, it becomes even more special.

Add to that its role as one of the last stands of coastal sage scrub habitat, and its tidepools and their role in the whole life cycle of the sea, and Cabrillo National Monument beckons the local resident and the visitor alike. For such a small park, Cabrillo National Monument offers an abundance of historical and natural resources for people to enjoy for generations to come.

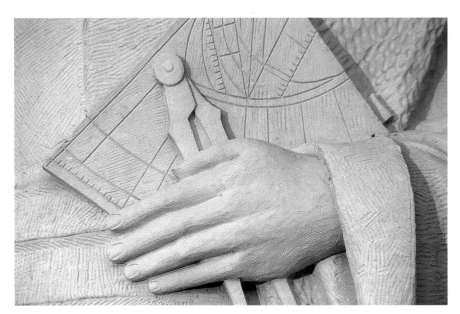

Cabrillo's navigation instruments emphasize the Monument's *commemoration of the exploration of the Americas.*

KC Publications has been the leading publisher of colorful, interpretive books about National Park areas, public lands, Indian lands, and related subjects for over 37 years. We have 6 active series—over 125 titles—with Translation Packages in up to 8 languages for over half the areas we cover. Write, call, or visit our web site for our full-color catalog.

Our series are:

The Story Behind the Scenery® – Compelling stories of over 65 National Park areas and similar Public Land areas. Some with Translation Packages.

in pictures... The Continuing Story® – A companion, pictorially oriented, series on America's National Parks. All titles have Translation Packages.

For Young Adventurers™ – Dedicated to young seekers and keepers of all things wild and sacred. Explore America's Heritage from A to Z.

Voyage of Discovery™ – Exploration of the expansion of the western United States.

Indian Culture and the Southwest – All about Native Americans, past and present.

Calendars – For National Parks and Southwest Indian culture, in dramatic full color, and a companion Color Your Own series, with crayons.

To receive our full-color catalog featuring over 125 titles—Books, Calendars, Screen Scenes, Videos, Audio Tapes, and other related specialty products:

Call (800-626-9673), fax (702-433-3420), write to the address below, Or visit our web site at www.kcpublications.com

Published by KC Publications, 3245 E. Patrick Ln., Suite A, Las Vegas, NV 89120.

Inside back cover:
Few sights in the region are as spectacular as the sunset lighting the water and the rocks at Cabrillo National Monument.

Back cover:
This is what sailors saw during the 36 years the lighthouse guided vessels into San Diego harbor.

Created, Designed, and Published in the U.S.A.
Printed by Tien Wah Press (Pte.) Ltd, Singapore
Color Separations by United Graphic Pte. Ltd